BY LARRY MACK

THE ATLANTA
FALCONS
STORY

BELLWETHER MEDIA · MINNEAPOLIS, MN

Are you ready to take it to the extreme? Torque books thrust you into the action-packed world of sports, vehicles, mystery, and adventure. These books may include dirt, smoke, fire, and chilling tales. : read at your own risk.

This edition first published in 2017 by Bellwether Media, Inc.

No part of this publication may be reproduced in whole or in part without written permission of the publisher. For information regarding permission, write to Bellwether Media, Inc., Attention: Permissions Department, 5357 Penn Avenue South, Minneapolis, MN 55419.

Library of Congress Cataloging-in-Publication Data

Names: Mack, Larry.
Title: The Atlanta Falcons Story / by Larry Mack.
Description: Minneapolis, MN : Bellwether Media, Inc., 2017. | Series:
   Torque: NFL Teams | Includes bibliographical references and index.
Identifiers: LCCN 2015050792 | ISBN 9781626173569 (hardcover : alk. paper)
Subjects: LCSH: Atlanta Falcons (Football team)—History—Juvenile literature.
Classification: LCC GV956.A85 M36 2017 | DDC 796.332/6409758231–dc23
LC record available at http://lccn.loc.gov/2015050792

Printed in the United States of America, North Mankato, MN.

TABLE OF CONTENTS

It is 20 to 0 at halftime. The Atlanta Falcons lead the Seattle Seahawks. This is their first **playoff** game following the 2012 season.

Matt Ryan

Jason Snelling

In the third quarter, the Seahawks score first. But the Falcons answer back. **Quarterback** Matt Ryan throws an easy pass to **running back** Jason Snelling. Touchdown!

Matt Bryant

Then Seattle scores 21 points in the fourth quarter. Now Atlanta is down by 1 point. Only 31 seconds are left in the game!

Again, Ryan takes charge. He leads the Falcons down the field. Then Matt Bryant kicks a 49-yard field goal. The Falcons win!

SCORING TERMS

END ZONE
the area at each end of a football field; a team scores by entering the opponent's end zone with the football.

EXTRA POINT
a score that occurs when a kicker kicks the ball between the opponent's goal posts after a touchdown is scored; 1 point.

FIELD GOAL
a score that occurs when a kicker kicks the ball between the opponent's goal posts; 3 points.

SAFETY
a score that occurs when a player on offense is tackled behind his own goal line; 2 points for defense.

TOUCHDOWN
a score that occurs when a team crosses into its opponent's end zone with the football; 6 points.

TWO-POINT CONVERSION
a score that occurs when a team crosses into its opponent's end zone with the football after scoring a touchdown; 2 points.

The Falcons took flight in the National Football League (NFL) in 1966. As an **expansion team**, they needed a name. The city of Atlanta held a contest.

A schoolteacher suggested "Falcons" for the fast, strong birds. Ever since, the team has tried to play like these brave birds of prey.

The Falcons have played home games in the Georgia Dome for more than 20 years. In 2014, Atlanta started building Mercedes-Benz Stadium for the 2017 season.

Features of the new stadium include huge glass walls and a roof that opens. The roof blooms like a flower!

BIG NUMBERS

A giant scoreboard was added around the hole in the new stadium's roof! It is 1,100 feet (335 meters) around!

ATLANTA, GEORGIA

GEORGIA DOME

N
W E
S

The Falcons play in the National Football **Conference** (NFC). Their **division** is the NFC South. The team was one of the first NFL teams in the southeastern United States. All of Atlanta's division **rivals** joined the league later. These teams are the Carolina Panthers, New Orleans Saints, and Tampa Bay Buccaneers.

NFL DIVISIONS

 AFC

AFC NORTH

 BALTIMORE **RAVENS**   CINCINNATI **BENGALS**

 CLEVELAND **BROWNS**   PITTSBURGH **STEELERS**

AFC EAST

 BUFFALO **BILLS**   MIAMI **DOLPHINS**

 PATRIOTS   NEW YORK **JETS**

AFC SOUTH

 TEXANS   INDIANAPOLIS **COLTS**

 JACKSONVILLE **JAGUARS**   TENNESSEE **TITANS**

AFC WEST

 DENVER **BRONCOS**   **CHIEFS**

 RAIDERS OAKLAND **RAIDERS**   SAN DIEGO **CHARGERS**

TOUGH DIVISION

In 2012, the Falcons only lost three regular-season games. Each loss was to a division rival.

NFC

NFC NORTH

 CHICAGO **BEARS**

 DETROIT **LIONS**

 GREEN BAY **PACKERS**

MINNESOTA **VIKINGS**

NFC EAST

 DALLAS **COWBOYS**

GIANTS

 PHILADELPHIA **EAGLES**

WASHINGTON **REDSKINS**

NFC SOUTH

 **FALCONS**

CAROLINA **PANTHERS**

 NEW ORLEANS **SAINTS**

 BUCCANEERS

NFC WEST

 CARDINALS

 LOS ANGELES **RAMS**

 SAN FRANCISCO **49ERS**

 SEATTLE **SEAHAWKS**

The Falcons struggled in the beginning. They did not have a **winning record** until 1971. It was their sixth year in the league.

The team made the playoffs for the first time in 1978. Then they did it again for the 1980 and 1982 seasons.

1971 season

The Falcons had one of their best regular seasons in 1998. The team lost just two games. Then they went all the way to **Super Bowl** 33.

SUPER BOWL 33
JANUARY 31, 1999

IN OVERTIME

The Falcons beat the Minnesota Vikings in overtime to reach Super Bowl 33. It was the first time an NFC Championship game went to overtime.

**NFC CHAMPIONSHIP
JANUARY 20, 2013**

The Falcons reached the NFC Championship game for the 2004 and 2012 seasons. But each time, they did not make it to the Super Bowl.

TIMELINE

1966

Played first
NFL season

1978

Made their first
appearance in the
playoffs

1992

First played at
the Georgia Dome

1980

Claimed first
division title

1971

Had their first season
with a winning record

Played in their first Super Bowl, but lost to the Denver Broncos

19   FINAL SCORE   **34**

Made it to the NFC Championship game for the 2012 season, but lost to the San Francisco 49ers (24-28)

Moved to Mercedes-Benz Stadium

Made it to the NFC Championship game for the 2004 season, but lost to the Philadelphia Eagles (10-27)

FALCONS

Quarterback Steve Bartkowski was an early superstar on the Falcons. He took the team to the playoffs for the first time. Star **center** Jeff Van Note **snapped** the ball to Bartkowski.

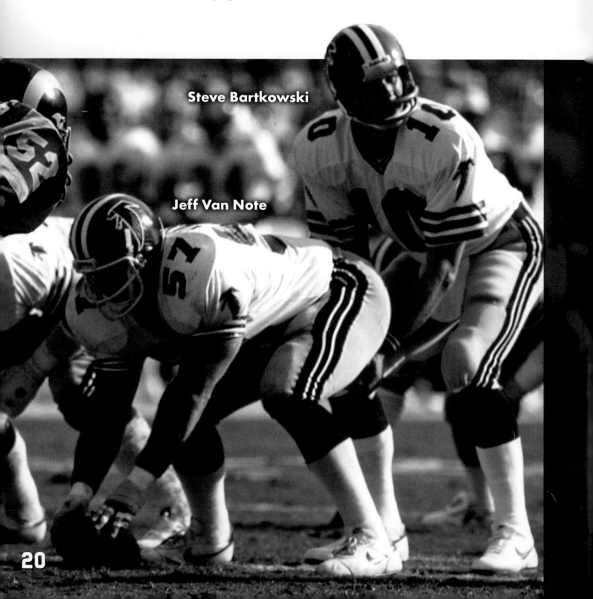

Steve Bartkowski

Jeff Van Note

Gerald Riggs

Morten Andersen

TOP NFL SCORER
Kicker Morten Andersen was a Falcon for part of his career. He is the top-scoring NFL player ever, with 2,544 total points!

In 1982, running back Gerald Riggs joined the **offense**. He became the team's all-time leading rusher. Tackle Mike Kenn often created room for Riggs to run.

Linebacker Jessie Tuggle was a Falcon for more than a decade. He was nicknamed "The Hammer" because of his tackling skills. **Cornerback** Deion Sanders was another weapon on **defense**. He was fast and could stop and steal passes.

Today, quarterback Matt Ryan is the man to watch. His very first NFL pass was for a touchdown!

TEAM GREATS

JEFF VAN NOTE
CENTER
1969–1986

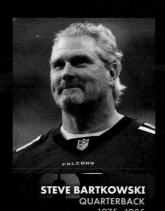

STEVE BARTKOWSKI
QUARTERBACK
1975–1985

MIKE KENN
OFFENSIVE TACKLE
1978–1994

Jessie Tuggle

GERALD RIGGS
RUNNING BACK
1982–1988

JESSIE TUGGLE
LINEBACKER
1987–2000

MATT RYAN
QUARTERBACK
2008–PRESENT

The Atlanta Falcons have many faithful fans. They dress in red and black. Many gather before home games to grill outside.

Some fans even march to the game together. The team mascot, Freddie Falcon, leads the parade. The team's drumline and cheerleaders also march along.

Freddie Falcon

During the game, fans wave flags as they cheer. Many have the words "Rise Up." Some players celebrate touchdowns with the "Dirty Bird." For this dance, they flap their arms and bounce around.

Dirty Bird

Both fans and players are ready for the Falcons to soar to another Super Bowl!

MORE ABOUT THE
FALCONS

Team name:
Atlanta Falcons

Team name explained:
Named after birds of prey called falcons

Nickname:
The Dirty Birds

Joined NFL: 1966

Conference: NFC

Division: South

Main rivals: Carolina Panthers, New Orleans Saints

Hometown:
Atlanta, Georgia

Training camp location:
XFINITY Training Camp,
Flowery Branch, Georgia

ATLANTA —○

GEORGIA

N
W ✛ E
S

Home stadium name:
Mercedes-Benz Stadium

Stadium opened: 2017

Seats in stadium: 71,000

Logo: A swooping
falcon shaped like the
letter F

Colors: Red and black

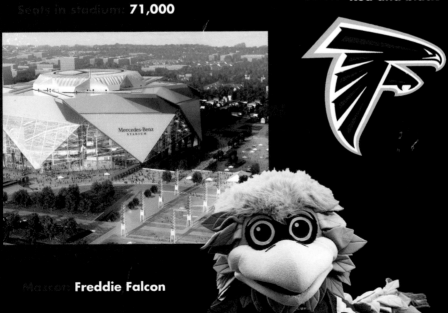

Mascot: Freddie Falcon

GLOSSARY

center—a player on offense whose main jobs are to snap the ball and block for teammates

conference—a large grouping of sports teams that often play one another

cornerback—a player on defense whose main job is to stop wide receivers from catching passes; a cornerback is positioned outside of the linebackers.

defense—the group of players who try to stop the opposing team from scoring

division—a small grouping of sports teams that often play one another; usually there are several divisions of teams in a conference.

expansion team—a new team added to a sports league

linebacker—a player on defense whose main job is to make tackles and stop passes; a linebacker stands just behind the defensive linemen.

offense—the group of players who try to move down the field and score

playoff—a game played after the regular NFL season is over; playoff games determine which teams play in the Super Bowl.

quarterback—a player on offense whose main job is to throw and hand off the ball

rivals—teams that are long-standing opponents

running back—a player on offense whose main job is to run with the ball

snapped—passed the ball backward to start an offensive play

Super Bowl—the championship game for the NFL

winning record—when a team has more wins than losses in a season

TO LEARN MORE

AT THE LIBRARY

Frisch, Nate. *The Story of the Atlanta Falcons.* Mankato, Minn.: Creative Education, 2014.

Monnig, Alex. *Atlanta Falcons.* Mankato, Minn.: Child's World, 2015.

Wyner, Zach. *Atlanta Falcons.* New York, N.Y.: AV2 by Weigl, 2015.

ON THE WEB

Learning more about the Atlanta Falcons is as easy as 1, 2, 3.

1. Go to www.factsurfer.com.

2. Enter "Atlanta Falcons" into the search box.

3. Click the "Surf" button and you will see a list of related web sites.

With factsurfer.com, finding more information is just a click away.

INDEX